Printed in the United States of America
www.aleishahdwrites.com

Daniel Fast Prayer Journal

21 Days of Scriptures & Guided Prayers

Aleisha H. Dubose

The Daniel Fast Food List

All fruit// fresh, frozen, juiced, or canned

Apples, apricots, bananas, cherries, grapes, lemons, limes, peaches, pineapples, strawberries, watermelon, etc.

All vegetables// fresh, frozen, dried, juiced, or canned

Asparagus, broccoli, cabbage, carrots, corn, cucumbers, lettuce, mushrooms, onions, potatoes, spinach, sweet potatoes, tomatoes, veggie burgers, etc.

All whole grains

Whole wheat, brown rice, millet, barely, oats, quinoa, grits, whole wheat pasta, whole wheat tortillas, rice cakes, popcorn, etc.

All nuts & seeds

Sunflower seeds, cashews, peanuts, sesame, nut butters (including peanut butter).

All legumes// canned or dried

Dried beans, pinto beans, split peas, lentils, black eyed peas, kidney beans, black beans, cannellini beans, white beans.

All quality oils

Olive, canola, grape seed, peanut, and sesame.

Beverages

Natural fruit juices, spring water, distilled water, other pure waters.

Others

Tofu, soy products, vinegar, seasonings, salt, herbs, spices.

Special Prayer Requests:

Special Prayer Requests:

Special Prayer Requests:

Special Prayer Requests:

Special Prayer Requests:

Day 1

Give thanks to the Lord, for He is good; His love endures forever.

1 Chronicles 16:34 (NLT)

Let's start by blessing God with our gratitude for all He has done in our lives. Thank Him for giving us yet another chance to get it right and live for Him.

What are some things you'd like to give God thanks for on today?

1.

2.

3.

4.

Prayer:

Day 2

Confess your sins to each other and pray for each other so that you may be healed. The earnest prayer of a righteous person has great power and produces wonderful results.

James 5:16 (NLT)

On today, make a list of friends and loved ones you would like to cover in prayer. This list can be as specific or general as you would like it to be.

1.

2.

3.

4.

5.

6.

7.

8.

9.

10.

Prayer:

Day 3

Create in me a clean heart, O God. Renew a loyal spirit within me.

Psalms 51:10 (NLT)

Pray this scripture over yourself today. Ask God to come and perform a system reboot on you, a recalibration, if you will. Allow Him to help you get reset and refocus your attention and energy on the mission He has set for your life.

Prayer:

Day 4

Dear friends, I warn you as "temporary residents and foreigners" to keep away from worldly desires that wage war against your very souls.

1 Peter 2:11 (NLT)

Think about some desires in your life that are not related to God nor do they glorify Him in any way. Evaluate those things and list them here. Then ask God to remove anything that isn't like Him or doesn't help propel the kingdom.

1.

2.

3.

4.

5.

Prayer:

Day 5

'Why have we fasted,' they say, 'and You do not see it? Why have we humbled ourselves and You do not notice?'

Hear this [O Israel], on the day of your fast [when you should be grieving for your sins] you find something you desire [to do], And you force your hired servants to work [instead of stopping all work, as the law teaches].

Isaiah 58:3 (AMP)

Assess your reasoning behind wanting to fast. Make sure you are aligned with God's will, word, and purpose. The point of fasting is not to get accolades and pats on the back, but for answered prayers and growing closer to God. Pray for God to touch your heart that you may have the right intentions going forward in this fast.

Prayer:

Day 6

This fulfilled the word of the Lord through the prophet Isaiah, who said, "He took our sicknesses and removed our diseases."

Matthew 8:17 (NLT)

O Lord my God, I cried to you for help, and you restored my health.

Psalms 30:2 (NLT)

Say a prayer for complete healing and comfort over all who are sick and afflicted. Ask that if it's God's will, He will give them peace during this time so that they might more easily endure their situation.

Prayer:

Day 7

He heals the brokenhearted and bandages their wounds.

Psalms 147:3 (NLT)

On this day think about all of those who are grieving. The pain that comes from the loss of a loved one can be difficult to navigate. Pray for comfort. Pray for peace. Pray for understanding. Pray that God keeps their minds intact while they are going through.

Prayer:

Day 8

And God will generously provide all you need. Then you will always have everything you need and plenty left over to share with others.

2 Corinthians 9:8 (NLT)

Pray for those in need of food, shelter, and other basic necessities that they will be able to see the hand of God at work in their lives when their needs are met. Pray that they find a community that will show them God's love, encourage them and help them draw closer to God.

Prayer:

Day 9

The Lord Most High is your fortress. Run to him for safety, and no terrible disasters will strike you or your home. God will command his angels to protect you wherever you go.

Psalms 91:9-11 (CEV)

Pray a prayer of protection over yourself and your loved ones. Pray that God will keep those who mean you harm far from you and surround you with people who have your best interest at heart. Also pray that God would shut the doors that you were not meant to walk through.

Prayer:

Day 10

Then, because you belong to Christ Jesus, God will bless you with peace that no one can completely understand. And this peace will control the way you think and feel.

Philippians 4:7 (CEV)

On this day, say a prayer for peace, not only for you but for those around you. Maybe you need peace in your home, at work, or even if it's just peace of mind that you desire. God can provide that for you. Write down all the areas in your life where you would like to have peace, then pray about them.

1.

2.

3.

4.

Prayer:

Day 11

Christ chose some of us to be apostles, prophets, missionaries, pastors, and teachers, so his people would learn to serve and his body would grow strong. This will continue until we are united by our faith and by our understanding of the Son of God.

Ephesians 4:11-13 (CEV)

Today, say a prayer for the leaders, both present and future, who are tasked with teaching and preaching the word of God to the masses. Pray their strength that they won't get weary while on this journey.

Prayer:

Day 12

I appeal to you, dear brothers and sisters, by the authority of our Lord Jesus Christ, to live in harmony with each other. Let there be no divisions in the church. Rather, be of one mind, united in thought and purpose.

1 Corinthians 1:10 (NLT)

Today, say a prayer for unity amongst the saints. Pray that we can come together as one body in order to glorify God and uplift his Kingdom.

Prayer:

Day 13

"But when you are praying, first forgive anyone you are holding a grudge against, so that your Father in heaven will forgive your sins too."

Mark 11:25 (NLT)

Today, say a prayer for forgiveness. Pray that God will touch your heart and soften it where it has grown hard. Pray that He will help you to release whatever it is that you may be harboring in your heart of hearts, both known and unknown, towards others.

Prayer:

Day 14

For we are God's masterpiece. He has created us anew in Christ Jesus, so we can do the good things he planned for us long ago.

Ephesians 2:10 (NLT)

"I knew you before I formed you in your mother's womb. Before you were born I set you apart and appointed you as my prophet to the nations."

Jeremiah 1:5 (NLT)

Today, go before the Lord in prayer about the expectations and purpose he has for you. Ask Him to show you what He would have you to do in order to enhance the Kingdom for His glory.

Prayer:

Day 15

But the wisdom from above is first of all pure. It is also peace-loving, gentle at all times, and willing to yield to others. It is full of mercy and the fruit of good deeds. It shows no favoritism and is always sincere.

James 3:17 (NLT)

Today, say a prayer for God to bless you with heavenly wisdom so you might continue on your journey to becoming more mature in your walk with him.

Prayer:

Day 16

"This is my command—be strong and courageous! Do not be afraid or discouraged. For the Lord your God is with you wherever you go."

Joshua 1:9 (NLT)

"So be strong and courageous! Do not be afraid and do not panic before them. For the Lord your God will personally go ahead of you. He will neither fail you nor abandon you."

Deuteronomy 31:6 (NLT)

Today say a prayer seeking courage. Several times in the Bible, we are asked to have courage. Pray that God will give you the courage you need to carry out His purpose and plans for your life. What are some situations in your life right now where you could use a little courage? Is it having the courage to speak the truth in love to friends or family members? Could it be the courage to speak up on your own behalf at work or home? Whatever this looks like for you, pray over these things as well.

Prayer:

Day 17

If you openly declare that Jesus is Lord and believe in your heart that God raised him from the dead, you will be saved.

Romans 10:9 (NLT)

Today say a prayer for all of your unsaved loved ones. Pray that they will come to God before it's too late. Also, if you are given the opportunity to speak with them on the matter, pray that God gives you the words to say that will encourage them to lean towards him.

Make a list of all of your unsaved relatives that you'd like to cover in prayer here:

1.

2.

3.

4.

6.

7.

8.

9.

10.

Prayer:

Day 18

For the Lord's sake, submit to all human authority—whether the king as head of state, or the officials he has appointed.

1 Peter 2:13-14 (NLT)

Everyone must submit to governing authorities. For all authority comes from God, and those in positions of authority have been placed there by God.

Romans 13:1 (NLT)

Today say a prayer for those serving in our government, both locally and nationally. Pray that they will uphold God's morals and standards. Also, pray that they do not lose sight of why they have been allowed to sit in the seat they are in.

Prayer:

Day 19

O God, you have ground me down and devastated my family.

Job 16:7 (NLT)

The Spirit of the Sovereign Lord is upon me, for the Lord has anointed me to bring good news to the poor. He has sent me to comfort the brokenhearted and to proclaim that captives will be released and prisoners will be freed.

Isaiah 61:1 (NLT)

Today say a prayer for all of the broken families. There are many reasons a family may be dealing with brokenness. Whether it be grief, jealousy, lies, or damaging secrets, whatever the case, God can fix it. Pray for a complete restoration of all families having to deal with these things.

Prayer:

Day 20

Now the Spirit of the Lord had left Saul, and the Lord sent a tormenting spirit that filled him with depression and fear.

1 Samuel 16:14 (NLT)

Worry weighs a person down; an encouraging word cheers a person up.

Proverbs 12:25 (NLT)

Today say a prayer for those struggling with anxiety and depression. Pray that they be released from these spirits so that they may live a more productive and fulfilling life, pleasing to God.

Prayer:

Day 21

But I say, love your enemies! Pray for those who persecute you!

Matthew 5:44 (NLT)

Bless those who curse you. Pray for those who hurt you.

Luke 6:28

Today say a prayer for all of your enemies, known and unknown. Don't let the fact that they dislike you or have wronged you determine how you pray. Pray that God will help you to love them with the love of Christ.

Prayer:

Reflection

Take this time to think back over the past couple of days or weeks. Have any of the prayers been answered? Are they in the middle of being answered? Has a situation changed since you began praying on it? If you're still waiting on a prayer to be answered, continue to pray even if this fast has ended. You may want to start a new fast. Be intentional about keeping the prayers going if you're still waiting on answers or waiting to see a shift in the situation. Use the next few pages to keep track of the answered prayers.

Meal & Snack Ideas

No Bake Peanut Butter Cookies:

1 cup Stevia

½ cup unsweetened vanilla almond milk

½ cup earth balance organic butter

¾ cups natural creamy peanut butter

1 tsp vanilla extract

3 ¼ cups quick-cooking oats

Strawberry & banana smoothie:

12 med strawberries

1 banana

2 Tbsp Stevia (honey)

1 cup unsweetened vanilla almond milk

My Version of a Chocolate Elvis:

1 cup unsweetened vanilla almond
milk

2 Tbsp all natural peanut butter

1 Tbsp of cocoa powder

1/2 banana

1 tsp vanilla extract

2 tsp Stevia

Note: This can also be made without the banana but if you cut the banana, make sure you also cut a Tbsp of the peanut butter.

Bean burrito:

Whole wheat tortilla

Hot sauce

Fresh spinach

Refried beans

Sauteed onions & peppers

Brown Rice w/ Sautéed Veggies:

1 medium onion

1 Bell pepper

1 pk Baby Bella Mushrooms

Brown rice (may also use whole grain rice)

sauté in olive oil and soy sauce and season to taste on medium heat

Meatless Spaghetti:

Pizza sauce or a no sugar added spaghetti sauce

1 medium onion

1 can diced tomatoes (can add a 2nd)

1 pack of Impossible ground beef (seasoned to taste)

1 box of whole grain, whole wheat, or rice noodles

Final Note:

I pray this prayer journal has been a beacon of guidance and comfort for all who embarked on its journey. If you were one who found fasting to be a daunting task, I hope this journal served to ease your mind and provided you with a solid foundation to start from. Be encouraged. Be blessed.

Aleisha H. Dubose

Made in the USA
Columbia, SC
04 June 2025

58746120R00043